CHANCE ENCOUNTERS

LESLEY COATES JONES

AMULET POETRY

First published in 2025

Amulet Poetry is part of ByTheBook
bythebook.press/amulet

Typesetting: ByTheBook
Print Management by Biddles Books, King's Lynn, Norfolk PE32 1SF

All rights reserved
© Lesley Coates Jones 2025

The moral right of Lesley Coates Jones to be identified as the author of this work has been asserted by her in accordance with Section 77 of the Copyright, Designs and Patents Act 1988

This book is sold subject to the condition that it shall not, by way of trade or otherwise, be lent, re-sold, hired out or otherwise circulated without the publisher's prior consent in any form of binding or cover other than that in which it is published and without a similar condition including this condition being imposed on the subsequent purchaser.

A CIP record for this book is available from the British Library

ISBN 978-1-917625-02-9

For Ken

*Our creativity, fired in the same crucible of love,
was a chance encounter to last a lifetime*

Poems

It Was All For You	11
Chiaroscuro	12
Lifetime	13
Bonds	14
Early	15
Scald	16
Forgiveness	18
St Matthew's	19
I Will Dream Dreams	20
Jumpin' Jack Flash	24
Willie Porter's Lad	25
Just a Goat	26
Catch	28
Endowed	29
Bramble	31
Pit Warrior	32
In Reverse Gear	34
Firstborn	35
All Things	36

In Our Green Shade	39
You Left Me Everything	42
Guitar	44
Fleet Angel	45
Trinity	46
With Such Dignity	49
In His Image	50
This Morning	52
First Snow	54
Wild Blooms	55
Ice Queen	58
God Doesn't Like It	59
I Carry Your Heart	60
In The End It's Only Love	61
In Tandem	62
Nuts and Bolts	64
Silhouette	67
Whispers	68

It Was All For You

It was all for you.
It was always
All for you.

Chiaroscuro

Even when the paint is stiff and inert on the brush
And words are captured in icicles…
Let me rejoice in chiaroscuro.
The tea is hot,
The girl delivering the medication calls a greeting.
Michaelmas chiaroscuros its petals
Against the carpeted copper ovals:
October's blessings, Harvest holiness.
Harlequin hides behind the misty gauze
Where frost has lain before it.
The last number of his contact is elusive
Yet his breath is soft on my cheek.
I caught just a glimpse of him as the door softly closed.
I thought I heard a thrush sing.
I thought I felt my soul spring
There in the last chink of light
Where chiaroscuro is least expected.
Laus Deo!
Chiaroscuro.

Lifetime

There was a time when
You couldn't face
Being alone.
And I needed an hour – or less even –
To paint and be
Me.
Now is the time when
Nothing would matter
If I could just hold your hand
For a few seconds more.
A lifetime, after all,
Was never going to be
Enough.

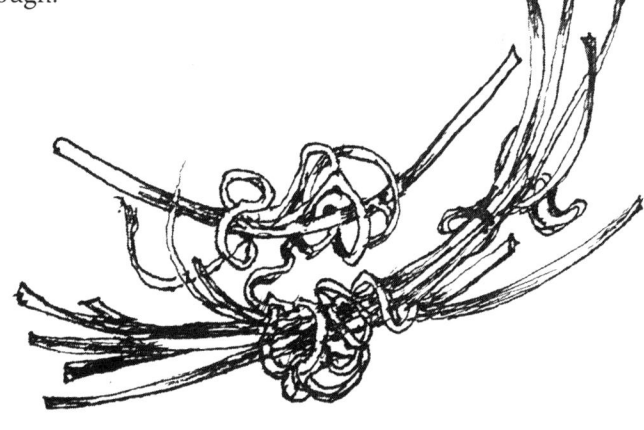

Bonds

How could such a small child know
The wrapped-round warmth of that?

The back of your cupped hand, stroking
The back of mine.
Devotion poured out without let or pause
Filling heart and soul with heaven's peace.

Child born on my day, your special day;
My love for you will never cease.

Early

The presence of the day creeps quietly
Into this sleeping valley,
Pink-tinged blankets of random clouds
Strewn across the hill-tops
Like the soft down on a young swan's neck
Whilst small birds, nesting still, in the
Creeping vine, welcome the subtle
Apricot light with busy chuntering twitter
And that moment, when all was still
Is over. It is over.
It is morning.

Scald

The first tea is almost
Too hot to drink.
I like it that way.
The sensation almost scalds my mouth.
It's a bitter-sweet assault on the tastebuds,
A suitable ritual to start the day.

My fingertips read my lover's work like braille,
Each luscious passage
With deep-cut message.
Fingerprints read and mark the story
Pain-filled shame and shining glory.
I caress each texture, as I so often
Would touch the skin of the slender hand
Of him who created miracles from raw pigment,
Rough cloth and fine sand.

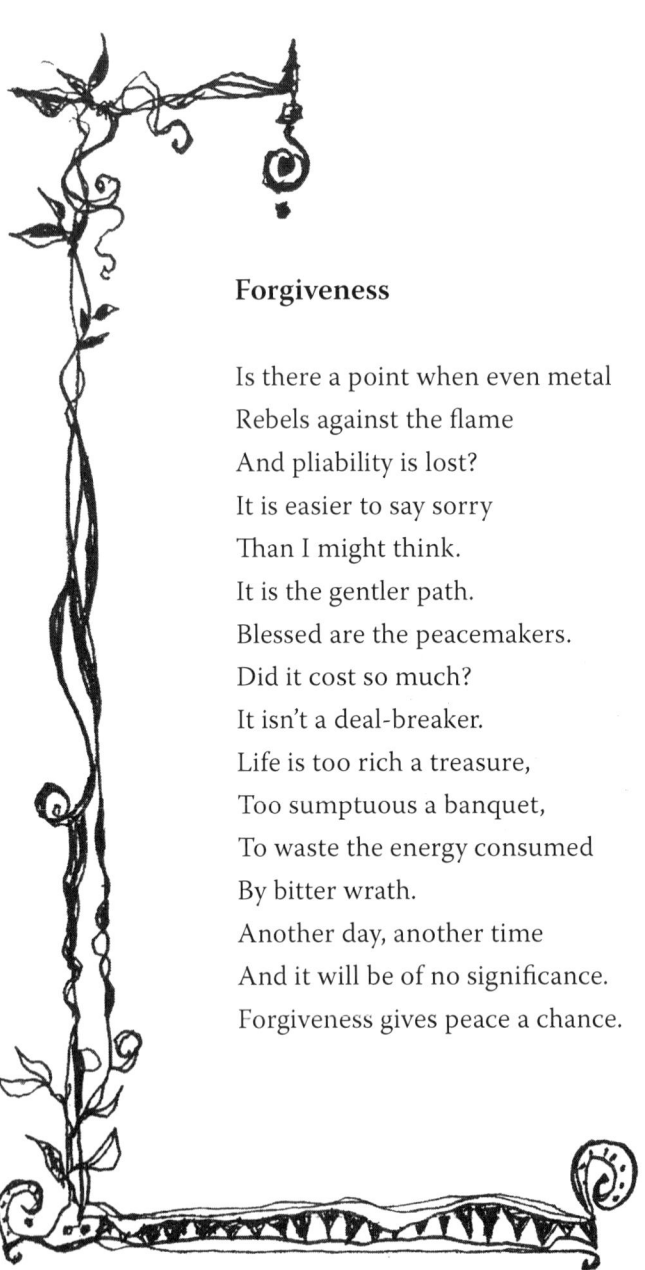

Forgiveness

Is there a point when even metal
Rebels against the flame
And pliability is lost?
It is easier to say sorry
Than I might think.
It is the gentler path.
Blessed are the peacemakers.
Did it cost so much?
It isn't a deal-breaker.
Life is too rich a treasure,
Too sumptuous a banquet,
To waste the energy consumed
By bitter wrath.
Another day, another time
And it will be of no significance.
Forgiveness gives peace a chance.

St Matthew's

Some thought it out of place
Too simple, too new.
Others thought it an architectural gem
With perfect form and structure.
The well-born, well-worn hands of old ones
Built it at the top of the hill, this time
Guarded by longhouse, lathe and rough places of rest.
A small, sacred shrine.
This place where, in this bleak season,
I fought my demons
And raged and roared and reasoned not,
Seeing only half-truths, wracked with angry, bitter thoughts
Until at last
Your still small voice
Said: She's still alive. Be glad of that!
And feathers and quills of angels at His word
Cooled my rage, and I was stilled
And warmed – and glad
Within these rough shapes
Of Yorkshire stones that gave
My spirit comfort.

I Will Dream Dreams

Does it take a message
In the night
To open up the truth?
To open it again?
Live the dream,
I tell them.
If you have things to do, do them.
Dream dreams.
We all need to swim with turtles
Before life hurtles
Us into more mundane paths and patterns.
Dream your dreams,
Make them happen.
Allow the world to take your breath away.
Live through the night.
Live through the day.

Be filled with awe and thankfulness.
It is yours.
This dream is yours.
Sheer wonder lies beneath the softest moss.
See that small enchantment.
Taste the vast rainbow of colour.
Live a colourful life.
Live your dreams,
Mark the stridulation of the cricket,
Uncover the hue behind the peeling paint.
Look again…
Turn stones over
Love your lover
Love your enemy
Live your life fully
Before it is over.

Jumpin' Jack Flash

We used to stiffen our petticoats with sugar water.
Nobody minded if it felt a bit sticky
When the night got so hot
And the hall doors were thrown open.
The brash, post-war swirling taffeta
Almost covered the candyfloss netting.
It could have been a setting
For Swan Lake.
In some ways, Doughty's Dance Hall
Was just as equal in its romance.
Hair sprayed big so it never moved a strand.
Three streets away they could hear the band.
Boys with legs as thin as sticks
Velvet collars, boots like bricks
Strict Methodist girls shared our lipsticks,
Bright pink slash – cut a dash
Jiving to Blue Suede Shoes and a quick whiff
From the Woodbine 'stache.

Willie Porter's Lad

He seemed such a shy, quiet boy
Until he'd had his fill at the King's Arms.
Then, it took very little persuasion
On any possible occasion
To get him to dance to 'The Stripper'
Right down to blue long-johns and slippers,
Entertaining wild, packed bars and tippers.

One partying night at home, he took the chain saw
To the wobbly kitchen table-legs
Before his mother had stormed from her bed.
She beat him so hard, he escaped to the shed.
She wept at the sight of the very short table.
Which still remained profoundly unstable.
A farmer's wife in a rage is a sight to behold,
Whilst he, in the hay, slept like the child
Who was always best beloved.

Just a Goat

Auntie Elsie's generous hand was warm,
Fat-fingered, carbolic-rough, with
Square-cut nails, and the smell of baking balm.
The mottled brown patterns over them
Once made me think she might become
A leopard – once her door had closed behind her.

It was her job to take me on that
First day to nursery.
A place saved just for me,
Though not yet three.
The door snapped shut behind me.
In front, a long, light, glass corridor.
Plants with bright red flowers lined the windows
To the square yard beyond – grey and plain.

Miss Dickinson gave me a tin mug,
A blanket for my bed, and showed me
The peg on which to hang my coat
All with my special symbol: a wild Billy goat.

Catch

The slender grass is cool green, criss-crossed
And patterning my vision.
Earth is curiously warm beneath us
With all those murmurings and indications
Of life, busily engaged
In simply living.
It is a time for silence
A time for concentration.
We are on a mission, have a vision.
Quiet, quiet, gentle, gentle
The sparkling water overlaps our fingers,
Small bejewelled fishes slide and linger.
He taught me the moment when to
Curl up those fingers, wrap around
Coloured cold scales.

He is mine
If I so choose
But my gift
Is to let him loose.

Endowed

The child of seven summers
Climbed the three wide smooth steps
Up to the door of the academic year.
An opening to all things new,
Whichever way the wind blew.
Brass plate, elbow-greased
Bright as a shining medal
Proclaiming its purpose.

'Wakefield Girls' High School
Endowed for young ladies.'

Brand new uniform criss-crossed
With massive knitted scarf,
Safety pin secured.
Deep breath
Deep thought:
Endowed…
So that is what I am to be now?
Pit-village kid will soon know how.

Bramble

Each October he took me to those hedgerows
Where the blackberries were fat as florins:
Loose, juice, lip-licking
Dark-red fruits of spiky brambles
Lined the baskets and bellies
Of the foraging tramplers.
Grandad's gnarled, scarred hands
Enfolded my small skinny fingers,
Assuring love
Offering care in ample abundance.
On some special days
There would be wild mushrooms too
To sizzle in the flat pan, balanced
On black-leaded stove, back home,
Whilst we warmed our toes.

Pit Warrior

In those days, he had several
Half pairs of wrecked specs
Hanging on the bed rail
Above his shiny head.
It was an unspoken mystery
Just why and when he had decided
It was the right time for him
To take to his bed.
A curious small-bladed knife,
Bedrail razor-sharpened,
Was used to cut the Ladies' Brown and Fine Old Twist
With care to fill the much-tamped pipe.
Smoke-filled room and strong sweet tea
Was his salvation.

But it didn't save Grandad's life.

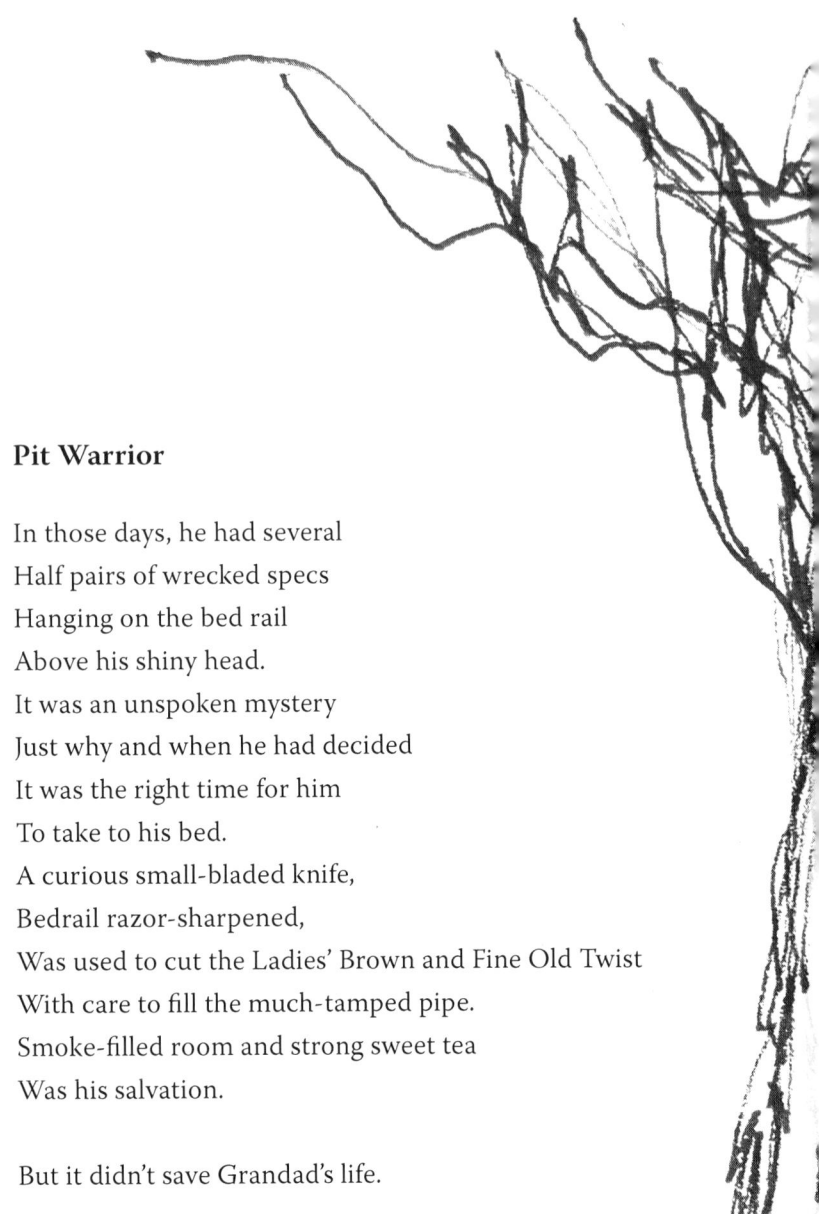

In Reverse Gear

All thrown into reverse.
It shouldn't be this way round.
The words play games with me,
Letters elude me, vowels fray my nerve endings.

Sleepy again, again, again.
Like a limp child – gentle Jesus
Meek and mild.
No fight left.
It's all right, they said. It's all right.
Let it be what it is, they said.
But I still remember and long for it to be other.

Words swing like a dead leaf on a spider's thread,
Mocking and mimicking my life's pendulum.
Spider's thread is so strong,
Life is too long
And yet, and yet, not long enough.
Tangled phrases, forgotten praises:
Lord have mercy. Christ have mercy.
Take me to tomorrow.
Take me the right way round.

Firstborn

In the halcyon days,
When his memory still served him,
He carved a head
For the saleroom rocking horse
Magnificent and strong
With reins and mane and tail to match.
Just for her, his first grandchild.
First of seven.
She sat astride the noble beast
Like some small majesty, so straight
And rocked with measured rhythmic beat.
Their eyes exchanged the smile that said it all
For this child there would be no defeat
Or he would know the reason why.
Life is full of do or die.

All Things

I must have got my coat-tail
Caught in yesterday's dream.
I never did move with any urgency
Except in a dire emergency.
Pain is devious; it creeps through cracks,
Like a mouse enters the house.
Sharp, needlepoint; double joint
Stretching skin, tight as a drum,
A crumb from His table… just a crumb,
Vice tight, dark night, no light.
Screws tighten,
Enough to frighten even a saint.
And that I'll never be.
Grace caught me, brought me self, in spider's spinning
As sure and pure as silver.

All things pass. All things pass.
Polished pendulum swings its rhythm,
Wheels roll day in, day out.
Too much sleeping; too much weeping.
An angel whispered in my ear.
It was like syncopated psalms to soothe
My soul.
All things pass. All things. All.

You were right,
of course...
It truly was our best summer
ever.

...though how could I know
how precious were those
warm sun-ripened hours
resting together
in our 'green thoughts'
in our 'green shade.'

In Our Green Shade

You were right,
Of course…
It truly was our best summer
Ever
…though how could I know
How precious were those
Warm, sun-ripened hours,
Resting together
In our 'green thoughts'
In our 'green shade'?

You Left Me Everything

You left me everything…
You left me the tools for living
Honed and sharpened to be safe and sure.
Dreams to last a thousand and one
Nights, or until I see you again.
Dreams of comfort and soft as the
Rose-petal touch of your slender hands.
Colours too, for every moment that
I miss you.
Shades beyond the painterly
Palette. Every hue a book
Of works in its own right.
You left me a saucerful of secrets
And an ocean full of tears
In eyes that kept the story closed.
You left me everything, except
What it felt like to be left.

You left me everything...
You left me the tools for living —
Honed and sharpened, to be safe
and sure.
Dreams to last a thousand and one
nights, or until I see you again.
Dreams of comfort and soft as the
rosepetal touch of your slender hands.
Colours too, for every moment that
I miss you...
Shades beyond the painterly
palette, every hue a book
of works in its own right
You left me a saucerful of secrets
and an ocean full of tears
in eyes that kept the story closed.
You left me everything, except
what it felt like
to be left.

Guitar

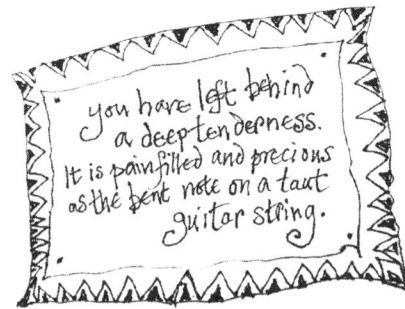

You have left behind
A deep tenderness
It is pain-filled and precious
As the bent note on a taut
Guitar string.

Fleet Angel

Hold fast the fleet angel
Lest love loses its grasp
And Harlequin puts on his last
Most perfect
Disguise.

Trinity

Three times three times three again
Began your poem, etched on my heart.
It rests there forever, a part
Of your creative legacy.

Now three trinities grace my life:
Spirit God made man to slay
Those wily demons, to feed the poor,
Heal wounds and pains,
Love man and beast,
Save our souls and love our foes.
To pray and praise, to share and care
And revel in his grand creation.

Above my head, when I'm in bed,
Three ancient Coptic crosses
Hang like keys to heaven
Intricate, unique, acknowledging my second trinity.

Three times three times three again:
Infinity defies an even number,
The florist's rule, small table's stability,
A sign that He does not sleep, nor even slumber.

The last of three sits on my lap,
Fur like silk and foxy face
Green eyes tight closed, my joy
And treasure, my affirmation.
Her name is Trinity
Because she only has three legs.

The Ancestors

With Such Dignity

Had this formidable matriarch really been
The runaway child-bride
All those many years ago?
How could anyone know?

One Christmas, after more port than he was used to,
Grandad had told May that,
And that they'd lost count of the children they had had,
In those days of bleak, unsupported childbirth.
And, oh, how they loved and cherished each other
And with timeless devotion cared for those
Little ones that did survive,
All with fancy names.
In her hats trimmed with exotic birds and feathers,
With such matriarchal dignity
She led us, the unlost ones of each generation
To Morning Prayer
In praise of God and Nation.

In His Image

I longed for you to know
Like I knew. How I longed.
I longed for so many futile years.
Perhaps my reasonings were unsupported
Tight-held hopes, cast out, aborted.
My moral code had no abode
Compared to your heart's empathy
It seemed a futile dream.
So when it came – not with a scream
Or some loud clatter of bells
But that small voice
So unobtrusively
There was no choice.
It was an unexpected epiphany
That you did not choose,
No, he chose you:
His magnificent creation
Made beautiful in His sight,
In His image!
Clean as a whistle, bright as a star,
Then, now forever, you still are
In His image.

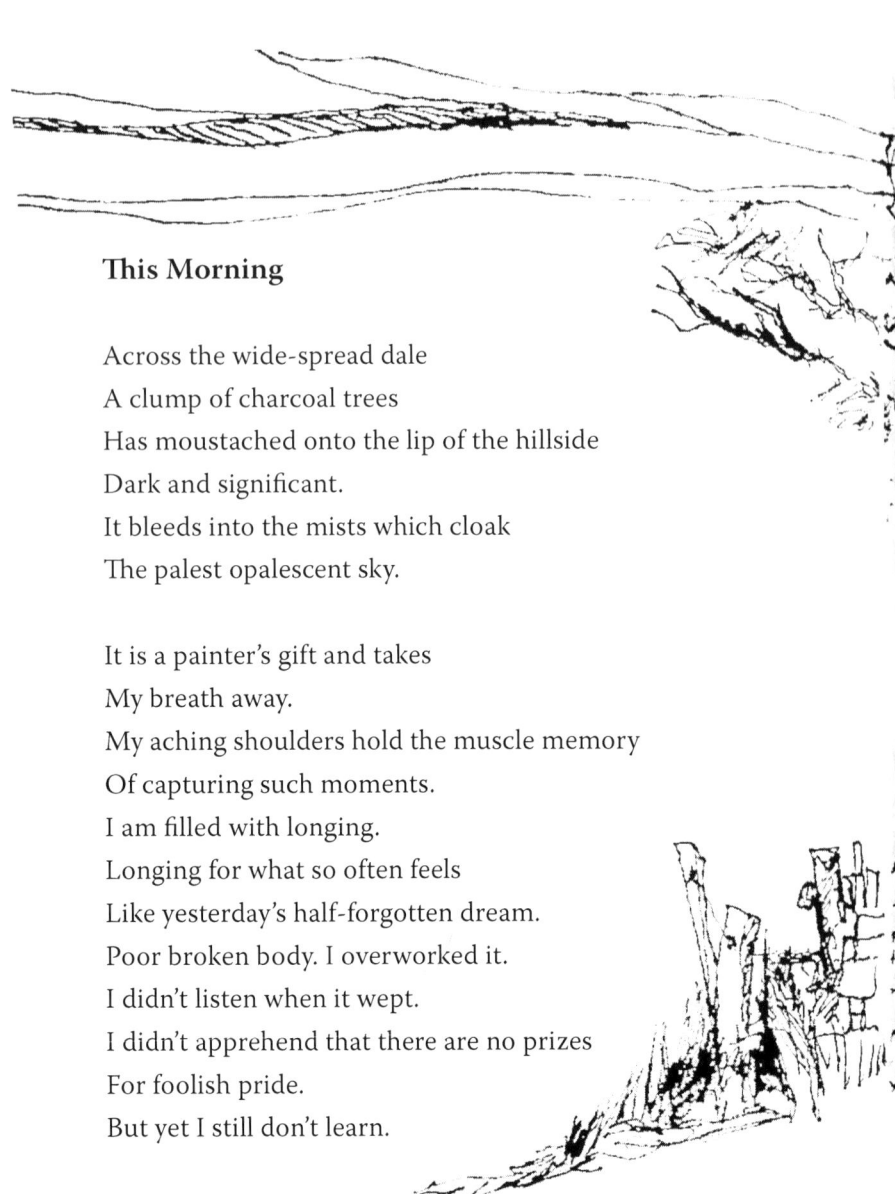

This Morning

Across the wide-spread dale
A clump of charcoal trees
Has moustached onto the lip of the hillside
Dark and significant.
It bleeds into the mists which cloak
The palest opalescent sky.

It is a painter's gift and takes
My breath away.
My aching shoulders hold the muscle memory
Of capturing such moments.
I am filled with longing.
Longing for what so often feels
Like yesterday's half-forgotten dream.
Poor broken body. I overworked it.
I didn't listen when it wept.
I didn't apprehend that there are no prizes
For foolish pride.
But yet I still don't learn.

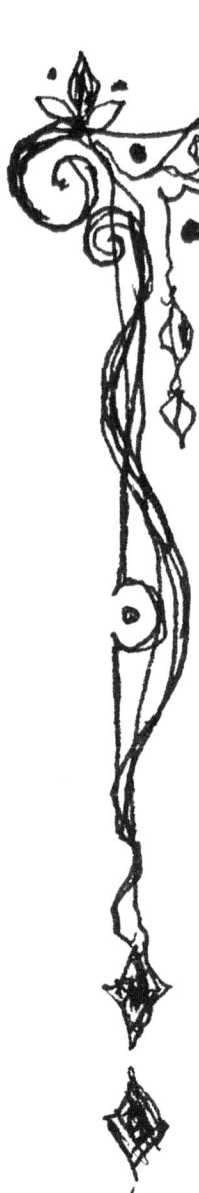

First Snow

White on sharp white
It came, as they said it would
Like an unbidden lost visitor
In search of bed and food.
It has adhered itself to lampposts,
Like some ardent lover;
It sits on iron rail, poised
As a cushioned velvet cover.
But it is only the fine, light stuff,
Here today, gone tomorrow.
Plush soft, it rests on roof,
Iron hard in farmer's furrow.

Wild Blooms

It was the last flower
To open its petals
Soft baby pink midst
Rose and button daisy.
Winter blooms blush
Bitter cold days with kisses
From afar. My friend never misses
Those unspoken days
When thin sun's rays
Creep into hearts of sorrow.
So hard to navigate.
Too tough to plough the furrow.
Hard-bitten frozen ruts
Jut under foot and wheel
Of my emotions.
My friend knows well these days.
She has a true, good heart.
The last flower to open.

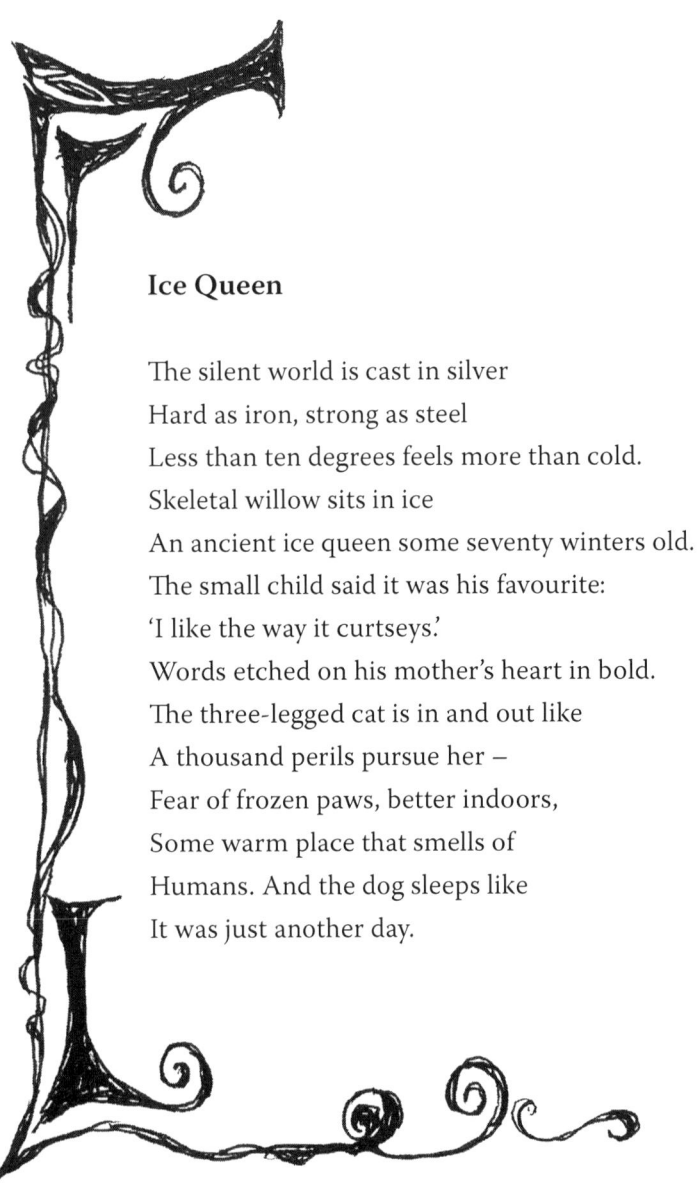

Ice Queen

The silent world is cast in silver
Hard as iron, strong as steel
Less than ten degrees feels more than cold.
Skeletal willow sits in ice
An ancient ice queen some seventy winters old.
The small child said it was his favourite:
'I like the way it curtseys.'
Words etched on his mother's heart in bold.
The three-legged cat is in and out like
A thousand perils pursue her –
Fear of frozen paws, better indoors,
Some warm place that smells of
Humans. And the dog sleeps like
It was just another day.

God Doesn't Like It

To assume the words
'My yoke is easy and my burden is light'
Make for a smooth, clear journey,
Is to underestimate man's devious wiles.
Self has to be challenged.
And that is not light, nor is it easy.

A true encounter with that which is greater,
A holy covenant with the Creator,
That is not light, nor is it easy.
And angels' messages
Dig deep in stubborn passages.
Do we have to hurt our friend, in love,
To help him heal?
Stick to the message laid on your heart.
That was the deal.
So by His Grace
And at His pace
The pain is healed in instant light
With both our hands clasped, prayer-tight.

I Carry Your Heart

I carry your heart like
A deep-cut diamond,
Facets piercing my chest,
Ever turning,
Reflecting our
Joys and sorrows.

In The End It's Only Love

'So may Your light shine before men.'

What greater joy than to love your heavenly Father?
But what is love?
God is love
Love is God
Give love when there's nothing left to give.

For words can fall on deaf ears
Words can be destroyed and changed.
Books are burned.
Mercy, joy, peace…
Only love is indestructible
Only love.

In Tandem

Even those perhaps inconsequential
Comments, reflections we shared –
So often – in tandem
As those do who
Are very close to each other
Are treasured like sacred jewels
In my heart.
They land like butterflies
In my soul.
At such unbidden moments
Our thoughts and instincts were
Enfolded in each other's delight.
Words to beguile
And weave their tender
Web that held us both
As one.

Nuts and Bolts

The die is loaded
Cards shuffled, stacked and dealt
With no due diligence.
No going back
And who would want to? No sense
In visiting that.
Good days, bad days – no proportion
No significance
Too loose, too tight in this skin that used to fit.

A month of days frayed at the edges,
Like a ragged, well-worn blanket,
And words and more words,
Clues to the plot or plan,
Trying to make sense of hearts or diamonds
And not a spade to be seen
To dig my way out.
I search for the place I once knew
But can't find it.

Not fit to see the light of day,
Yokes and burdens and a tongue
Coated with black pepper.
No spit, even teeth tremble
Against the time.
Ritual assemble,
Fill the plastic trough with water
Set machine, map jaw and cheek bones,
Fit the mask.
Fumble to get the tubes attached.
Shuffle face
To comfy place
And that's a laugh! Switch on
The noise of mimicked heartbeat
Which keeps me alive
And softens my sorrow
Until tomorrow.

Silhouette

I woke up again.
Am I just a silhouette
A soon-to-be shadow
Of myself?
I am weary of rehearsing
Each vile indignity.
How many leaves left to strip from
The human artichoke?
How much time to visit the poem
Which shaky hands manage somehow?
Still the curved instinctive line.
And she comes home to hold my hand,
Pairing together the bond that binds us.
To feed each other's creativity
Is an act of holy grace.
To hear her laughter fills my soul
And helps me forget the night
Terrors of cloned marching men with no eyes
And daylight hallucinations of
The unspeakable.
There is something to thank my
Creator for in each new dawn.
I know my pain is less than many.
Be with me my Redeemer,
Comfort me with your still, small voice.

Whispers

Gauze as fine and thin as a moth's wing
Separates us now.
Impenetrable. Unreadable.
A whisper of no substance.
Though you hide in midnight's doorway,
No plan or map to guide a way,
I know it's just a chance
Encounter that continues to surprise
And therein lies the true treasure.

Acknowledgements

Thank you to all, both living and dead, who have made this book possible.

To Jill Glenn and Claire Steele at ByTheBook, for their wisdom, encouragement and diligent attention to detail.

To my children, Duncan and Heather, and Claire and Kevin, for their love and support and immense, consistent enjoyment of my work.

To my seven grandchildren, who have kept me constantly loved, renewed and reinvented, and to my small great-grandchild, who claims me as her best friend.

To all my many friends, who have each added their valuable input into and support for my continued need to create.

To my friends at St Matthew's and St Andrew's Churches, who have wrapped me in prayer.

To all those who fight to love their enemy and engage themselves in love, laughter and creativity.

At ByTheBook, we are dedicated to discovering new creative talent and publishing beautiful books that will find their ways into the hearts of readers worldwide.

– AMULET POETRY –
BYTHEBOOK.PRESS